HAPP_ _ _ _ _ _ _!

(name of person receiving book)

Get ready for a super fun trip down memory lane! Inside this book, you'll find activities designed to spark smiles as you travel back in time.

We'll revisit trendy styles and pop culture from your era with some friendly trivia. You'll get to journal about monumental events and where you were when they happened. We'll reflect on your favorite moments both big and small - everything that's shaped your life story.

Go at your own pace, writing or just thinking about the good times. Stick in photos that capture memories. Most importantly, have fun reliving it all!

Your memories and wisdom need to be shared. Future generations would love to learn from your experiences. So grab a comfy seat and a nice pen, and start your stroll down memory lane. Everything about you is worth remembering.

CHEERS TO SEVENTY!

From Numbers to Narratives: 70 Years of Living!

70 TRIPS AROUND THE SUN
840 MONTHS
3,640 WEEKS
25,550 DAYS
2,207,520,000 SECONDS

Go ahead and calculate these for yourself!

Number of homes lived in.. ☐

Number of times fallen in love... ☐

Number of cars owned... ☐

Number of jobs.. ☐

Number of schools attended.. ☐

Number of pets loved... ☐

Number of languages learned.. ☐

Number of countries visited... ☐

Number of states visited.. ☐

Where Were You?

Where were you and what were you doing during these momentous events?

1. Assassination of John F. Kennedy (1963):

2. Assassination of Martin Luther King Jr. (1968):

3. Moon landing (1969):

4. Resignation of President Nixon (1974):

5. Fall of Saigon (1975):

6. Challenger Explosion (1986):

7. Fall of Berlin Wall (1989):

8. Princess Diana's Death (1997):

9. 9/11 Attacks (2001):

10. Election of First Black president (2008):

What other events are seared in your memory?

Short & Sweet

✦ 20 Questions ✦

1. Full name: _____
2. Place of birth: _____
3. Number of siblings: _____
4. First time to see the ocean: _____
5. First book you remember: _____
6. First vacation: _____
7. First meal you learned to cook: _____
8. First fast food restaurant: _____
9. First pet: _____
10. First movie you remember: _____
11. First best friend: _____
12. First boy/girl went steady with: _____
13. First kiss: _____
14. First love: _____
15. First plane ride: _____
16. First car: _____
17. First job: _____
18. First concert attended: _____
19. First home: _____
20. First big item you saved up to purchase: ____

Short & Sweet

✦ 20 Favorites ✦

1. Favorite decade: _____
2. Favorite family vacation: _____
3. Favorite games as a child: _____
4. Favorite movie: _____
5. Favorite classic car: _____
6. Favorite meal: _____
7. Favorite dessert: _____
8. Favorite hairstyle: _____
9. Favorite tv show: _____
10. Favorite candy: _____
11. Favorite teacher: _____
12. Favorite book: _____
13. Favorite quote: _____
14. Favorite job: _____
15. Favorite scent: _____
16. Favorite age: _____
17. Favorite holiday: _____
18. Favorite family story: _____
19. Favorite childhood song: _____
20. Favorite dance craze: _____

FASHIONISTA

How many different fashion trends did you rock?

Late 1960s (Ages 12-18):

___ **Mod Fashion:** Bold geometric patterns, A-line dresses, and go-go boots, reflecting the youthful energy of the era.
___ **Hippie Movement Beginnings:** Bell-bottom jeans and tie-dye shirts
___ **Mini Skirts:** A symbol of women's liberation and fashion innovation.
___ **Beatlemania Influence:** Slim-cut suits and mop-top haircuts.

Early to Mid-1970s (Ages 16-22):

___ **Disco Fashion:** Shiny fabrics, bell-bottom trousers, platform shoes and halter tops reflect the disco music scene.
___ **Flower Power:** Floral patterns persist, now more prominently featured in both women's and men's fashion.
___ **Leisure Suits:** Pastel colors or with bold prints.
___ **Fringed Vests and Earth Tones:** Influenced by the hippie aesthetic.

Late 1970s to Early 1980s (Ages 24-30):

___ **Punk Fashion:** Ripped jeans, leather jackets, and band T-shirts as a response to the mainstream disco style.
___ **New Wave and Glam Rock:** Bold colors, glam makeup, and eccentric clothing inspired by musicians like David Bowie.
___ **Power Dressing:** The emergence of the business suit for women.
___ **Athletic Wear as Daywear:** Tracksuits and sneakers start becoming popular as everyday fashion, influenced by the growing fitness craze.
___ **Designer Jeans:** A status symbol, often featuring prominent logos.
___ **Urban Cowboy:** Western wear sees a resurgence in popularity.

Late 1980s to Mid-1990s (Ages 34-40):

___ **Grunge Style:** Characterized by flannel shirts, ripped jeans, and combat boots, reflecting the influence of grunge music bands like Nirvana.
___ **Hip-Hop Influence:** Baggy jeans, branded sportswear, baseball caps, and sneakers become popular, influenced by the rising hip-hop culture.
___ **Rave Culture:** Bright, neon colors, baggy pants, and graphic tees influenced by the electronic music and rave scene.

___ **TOTAL** *Which fashion trends do you wish were still around today?*

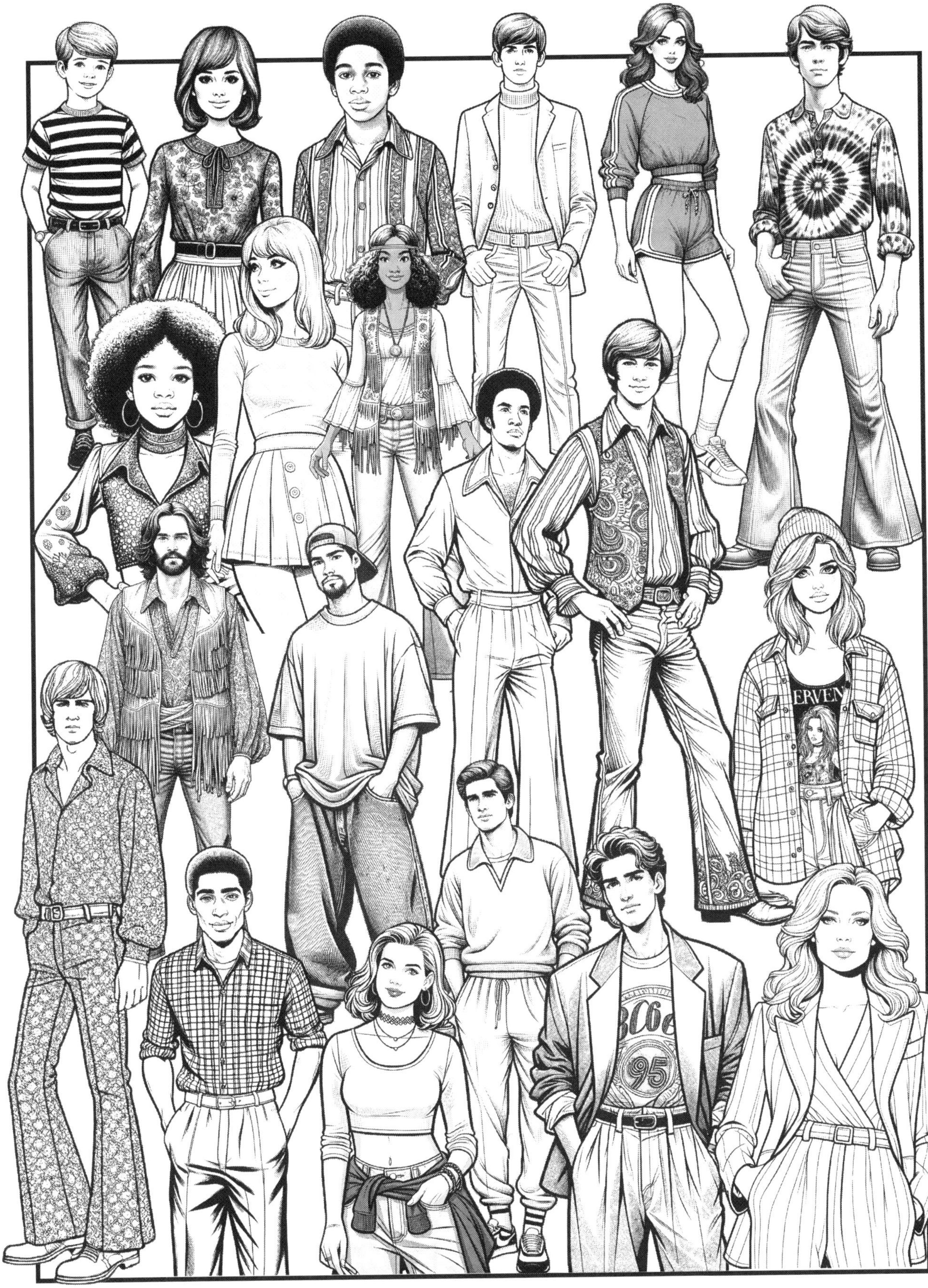
ERVEN
95

HAIRSTYLES

How many of these hairstyles have you had?

1960s (Childhood to Ten Years):
___ **Bowl Cut:** Easy-to-maintain cut that was prevalent in this era.
___ **Pigtails and Braids:** Often adorned with ribbons and bows.
___ **The Beatles' Mop-Top:** Tousled, bowl-like appearance.

1970s (Teens to 20s):
___ **Shag Hairstyle:** Layered and feathered like celebrities Fonda and Stewart.
___ **Afro:** A powerful statement of identity and pride.
___ **Long, Straight Hair:** Often worn with a center part in the hippie style.
___ **Feathered Hair:** Soft layers that are brushed back in a Farrah Fawcett style.
___ **Cornrows and Braids:** Popular within African-American communities.

1980s (20s to 30s):
___ **Big Hair:** Perms, teasing, and generous use of hairspray.
___ **Hi-top Fade:** A striking and bold style.
___ **Permed Hair:** Added volume and curls were all the rage with men and women.
___ **Mullets:** Business-like at the front and party at the back.
___ **Jheri Curl:** A glossy, loosely curled look that became widely adopted.

1990s (30s to 40s):
___ **The Rachel:** Inspired by Jennifer Aniston's character on "Friends."
___ **Grunge Hair:** Tousled, often unkempt hairstyles.
___ **Crew Cut and Buzz Cut:** A return to minimalist, low-maintenance styles.
___ **Box Braids and Twists:** Seen on celebrities like Brandy and Janet Jackson.

2000s (40s to 50s):
___ **Spiky Hair:** Often styled with gel for a textured, edgy look.
___ **Sleek and Straight:** Flat-ironed hair becomes a trend.
___ **Highlights and Frosted Tips:** Select strands are colored to contrast with the natural hair color.
___ **Bob Cut:** Classic bob cut with variations like the asymmetrical bob.

___ **Total** *Which hairstyle was your favorite?* _____

-9-

Have You Ever?

Check off the items you have done.

- ☐ Visited a World's Fair
- ☐ Learned an instrument
- ☐ Gone scuba diving
- ☐ Fallen in love
- ☐ Been to a sock hop
- ☐ Ridden in a hot air balloon
- ☐ Sold items door to door
- ☐ Participated in a protest
- ☐ Run a marathon
- ☐ Started a car with a crank handle
- ☐ Lived abroad
- ☐ Watched a soap box derby race
- ☐ Gone backpacking
- ☐ Worn a zoot suit or a poodle skirt
- ☐ Seen the northern lights
- ☐ Hitchhiked or picked up a hitchhiker
- ☐ Danced the funky chicken
- ☐ Learned another language
- ☐ Had a milkman deliver dairy products to your home
- ☐ Volunteered
- ☐ Ridden a steam locomotive train
- ☐ Traveled in a propeller-driven airplane
- ☐ Attended a Beatles concert
- ☐ Danced to Elvis Presley playing on a jukebox
- ☐ Fought in a war
- ☐ Attended a live radio broadcast

Would You Rather?

Make your choices and then grab a friend or family member and ask them these questions to see how well they know you.

◯ Wake up early	**OR**	Stay up late ◯
◯ Go shopping	**OR**	Shop online ◯
◯ Read a book	**OR**	Watch movie ◯
◯ Drink coffee	**OR**	Drink tea ◯
◯ Go to a party	**OR**	Quiet evening at home ◯
◯ Go on a cruise	**OR**	Go camping ◯
◯ Ice cream	**OR**	Pie ◯
◯ Cat person	**OR**	Dog person ◯
◯ Play board games	**OR**	Watch TV ◯
◯ Beach	**OR**	Mountains ◯
◯ Call	**OR**	Text ◯
◯ Travel the world	**OR**	Explore locally ◯

The Price is Right

How much did things cost back in 1955? Circle your best guess.

Avg. Wage/Year
a) $4,137
b) $2,000
c) $8,500

New Home
a) $5,500
b) $15,300
c) $10,950

Loaf of Bread
a) $0.50
b) $1.00
c) $0.18

Gold/Ounce
a) $200
b) $35
c) $10

Gallon of Gas
a) $0.23
b) $0.55
c) $0.10

Harvard Tuition
a) $2,000
b) $400
c) $800

Dozen Eggs
a) $0.10
b) $0.27
c) $1.75

Postage Stamp
a) $0.05
b) $0.03
c) $0.10

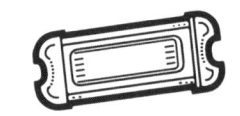

A Movie Ticket
a) $1.25
b) $0.10
c) $0.75

costs are average estimates (check your answers on page 38)

YOUNGER OR OLDER?

Do you think you're younger or older than these inventions?

		Younger	Older
1	**Microwave oven**	○	○
2	**Tupperware**	○	○
3	**Rubiks Cube**	○	○
4	**Mr. Potato Head**	○	○
5	**Color TV**	○	○
6	**Frisbee**	○	○
7	**Helicopter**	○	○
8	**Hula Hoop**	○	○
9	**Laser**	○	○
10	**Car Seat Belts**	○	○
11	**Barbie Doll**	○	○
12	**Credit Card**	○	○
13	**Monopoly Board Game**	○	○
14	**Electric Guitar**	○	○
15	**Sliced Bread**	○	○

(check your answers on page 39)

WORD SEARCH

N	S	Y	N	X	M	V	B	E	H
J	P	H	S	A	C	I	E	Y	U
U	U	T	P	E	T	C	A	N	L
K	T	R	E	L	C	W	T	A	A
E	N	A	L	Y	G	A	L	T	H
B	I	C	V	N	B	H	E	O	O
O	K	C	I	I	U	E	S	P	O
X	J	M	S	V	E	C	A	E	P
T	E	L	E	V	I	S	I	O	N
H	K	C	O	T	S	D	O	O	W

ELVIS **NATO** **PEACE**
MCCARTHY **WOODSTOCK** **HULA HOOP**
TELEVISION **BEATLES** **VINYL**
HEMINGWAY **JUKEBOX** **SPUTNIK**

-14- (check your answers on page 40)

GUESS THE MOVIE

Draw a line to match the movie each quote comes from.

"You see, in this world, there's two kinds of people, my friend: Those with loaded guns, and those who dig. You dig."

On the Waterfront, 1954

The Good, the Bad and the Ugly, 1966

"I coulda been a contender."

Ferris Bueller's Day Off, 1986

"Hasta la vista, baby."

Taxi Driver, 1976

"Life moves pretty fast. If you don't stop and look around once in a while, you could miss it."

Terminator 2: Judgment Day, 1991

"You talkin' to me?"

Dr. Strangelove, 1964

"If you build it, they will come."

The Graduate, 1967

"Here's to you, Mrs. Robinson."

Cool Hand Luke, 1967

"What we've got here is failure to communicate."

Field of Dreams, 1988

"Gentlemen, you can't fight in here! This is the War Room!"

-15- *(check your answers on page 41)*

Born in 1955

True or false. Guess which people were born in 1955.

		True	False
1	Bruce Willis	○	○
2	Kevin Costner	○	○
3	Bill Murray	○	○
4	Bill Nye	○	○
5	Stevie Wonder	○	○
6	Whoopi Goldberg	○	○
7	Sharon Stone	○	○
8	Steve Jobs	○	○
9	Liam Neeson	○	○
10	Whoopie Goldberg	○	○
11	Reba McEntire	○	○
12	Eddie Van Halen	○	○
13	Hillary Clinton	○	○
14	Dolly Parton	○	○
15	John Grisham	○	○

(check your answers on page 42)

1950s SLANG

Draw a line to match.

1. **Fat city**
2. **Burn rubber**
3. **Knuckle sandwich**
4. **Made in the shade**
5. **Pad**
6. **Blast**
7. **Shoot the breeze**
8. **Out to lunch**
9. **Peepers**
10. **Real gone**
11. **Jet**
12. **Square**
13. **Drag**
14. **Razz my berries**
15. **Flip your wig**

To drive away quickly

A state of great success

A house or home

Something that's boring

Glasses or spectacles

Suggesting someone has it easy

Having a great time

Very much in love

A playful threat of a punch

To chat casually without purpose

Someone who's clueless

Describing someone as unhip

To excite or impress someone

To leave quickly

To become very excited or go crazy

(check your answers on page 43)

Color in the states you have visited.

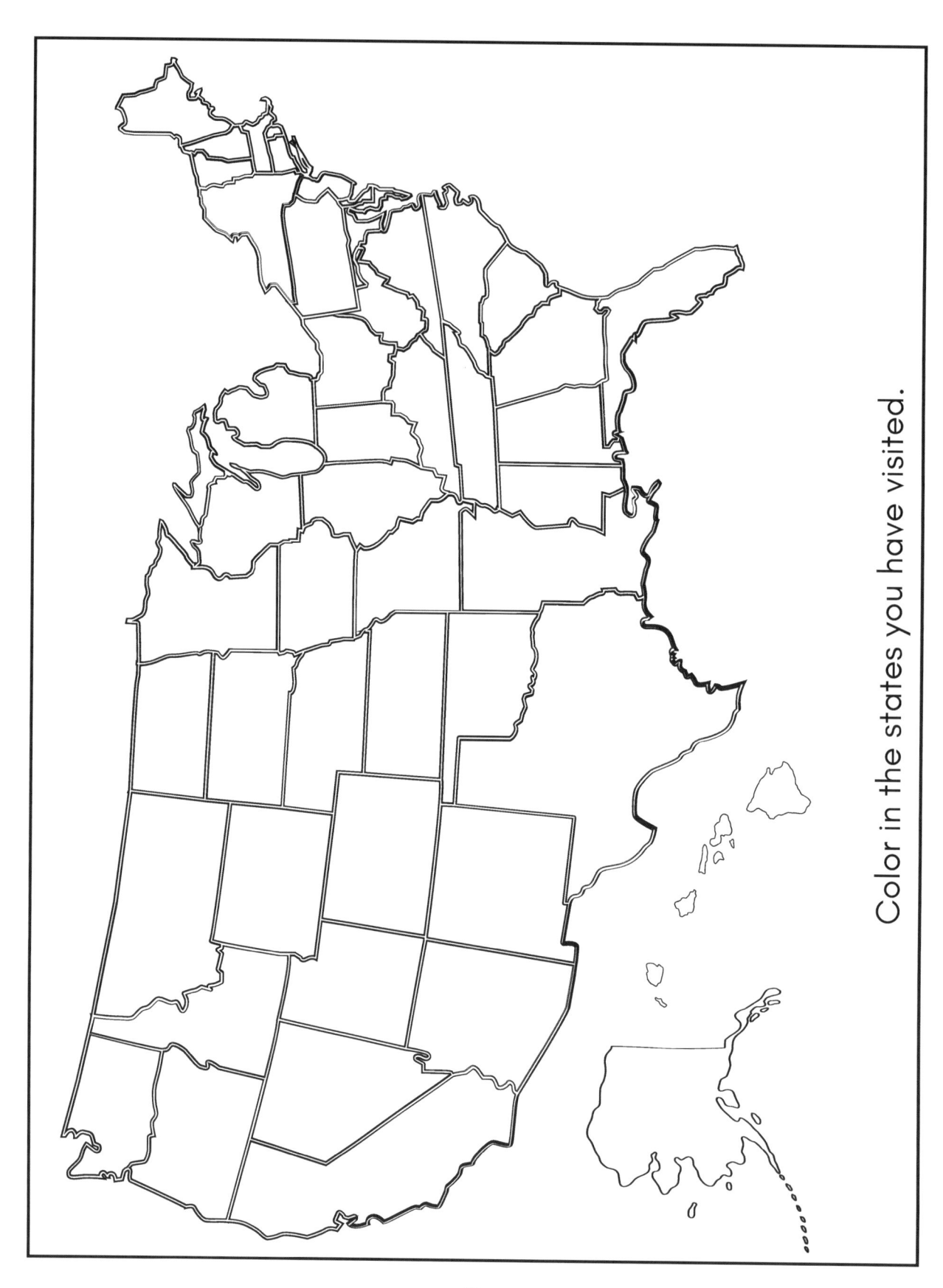

Color in the countries you have visited.

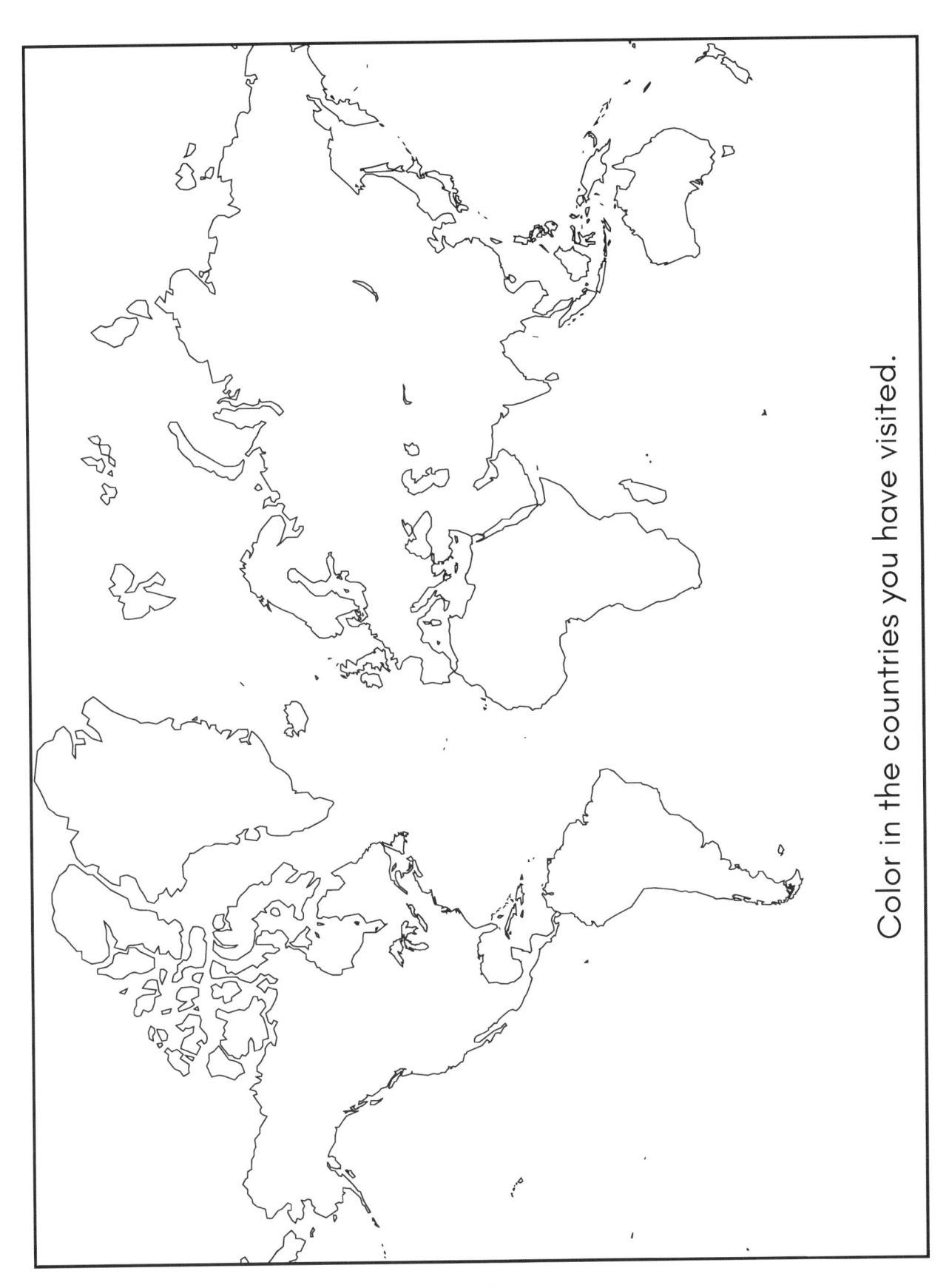

TRAVEL

When: .... Where: ....

Who was with you: ....

Things you saw: ....

....

....

Things you did: ....

....

....

One part of the trip you *wish* you could repeat: ....

When: .... Where: ....

Who was with you: ....

Things you saw: ....

....

....

Things you did: ....

....

....

One part of the trip you *wish* you could repeat: ....

TRAVEL

When: .... Where: ....

Who was with you: ....

Things you saw: ....

....

....

Things you did: ....

....

....

One part of the trip you *wish* you could repeat: ....

When: .... Where: ....

Who was with you: ....

Things you saw: ....

....

....

Things you did: ....

....

....

One part of the trip you *wish* you could repeat: ....

TRAVEL

When: .... Where: ....

Who was with you: ....

Things you saw: ....

....

....

Things you did: ....

....

....

One part of the trip you *wish* you could repeat: ....

When: .... Where: ....

Who was with you: ....

Things you saw: ....

....

....

Things you did: ....

....

....

One part of the trip you *wish* you could repeat: ....

TRAVEL

When: .... Where: ....

Who was with you: ....

Things you saw: ....

....

....

Things you did: ....

....

....

One part of the trip you *wish* you could repeat: ....

When: .... Where: ....

Who was with you: ....

Things you saw: ....

....

....

Things you did: ....

....

....

One part of the trip you *wish* you could repeat: ....

Challenge

Quick recall - no searching for answers!

How many Elvis Presley songs can you name?

How many of Liz Taylor's husbands can you name?

How many wars from when you were born to now can you name?

How many different dance crazes from the past can you recall attempting?

How many countries can you name that changed their names in your lifetime?

How many Vice Presidents from when you were born to now can you name?

How many classic TV shows from the 60s and 70s can you name?

How many music legends who performed at Woodstock can you name?

How many famous musicals from your era can you name?

Head to the internet to dive deeper and check your answers!

Finish the Sentence

Do your best to finish the lyrics of these iconic songs.

"You ain't nothin' but a hound dog, _____."
- Elvis Presley (1956)

"Imagine there's no heaven, _____."
- John Lennon, "Imagine" (1971)

"All you need is love, _____." - The Beatles (1967)

"Hey Jude, don't _____. Take a sad song and make it better." - The Beatles (1968)

"You're so vain, you probably _____."
- Carly Simon (1972)

"We will, we will _____." - Queen, "We Will Rock You" (1977)

"Don't stop believing, _____." - Journey (1981)

"Every breath you take, _____, I'll be watching you."
- The Police, "Every Breath You Take" (1983)

"Wake me up _____, don't leave me hanging on like a yo-yo." - Wham! (1984)

"I want to dance with somebody, _____ with somebody." - Whitney Houston (1987)

-25-   *(check your answers on page 44)*

How many different vehicles have you owned?

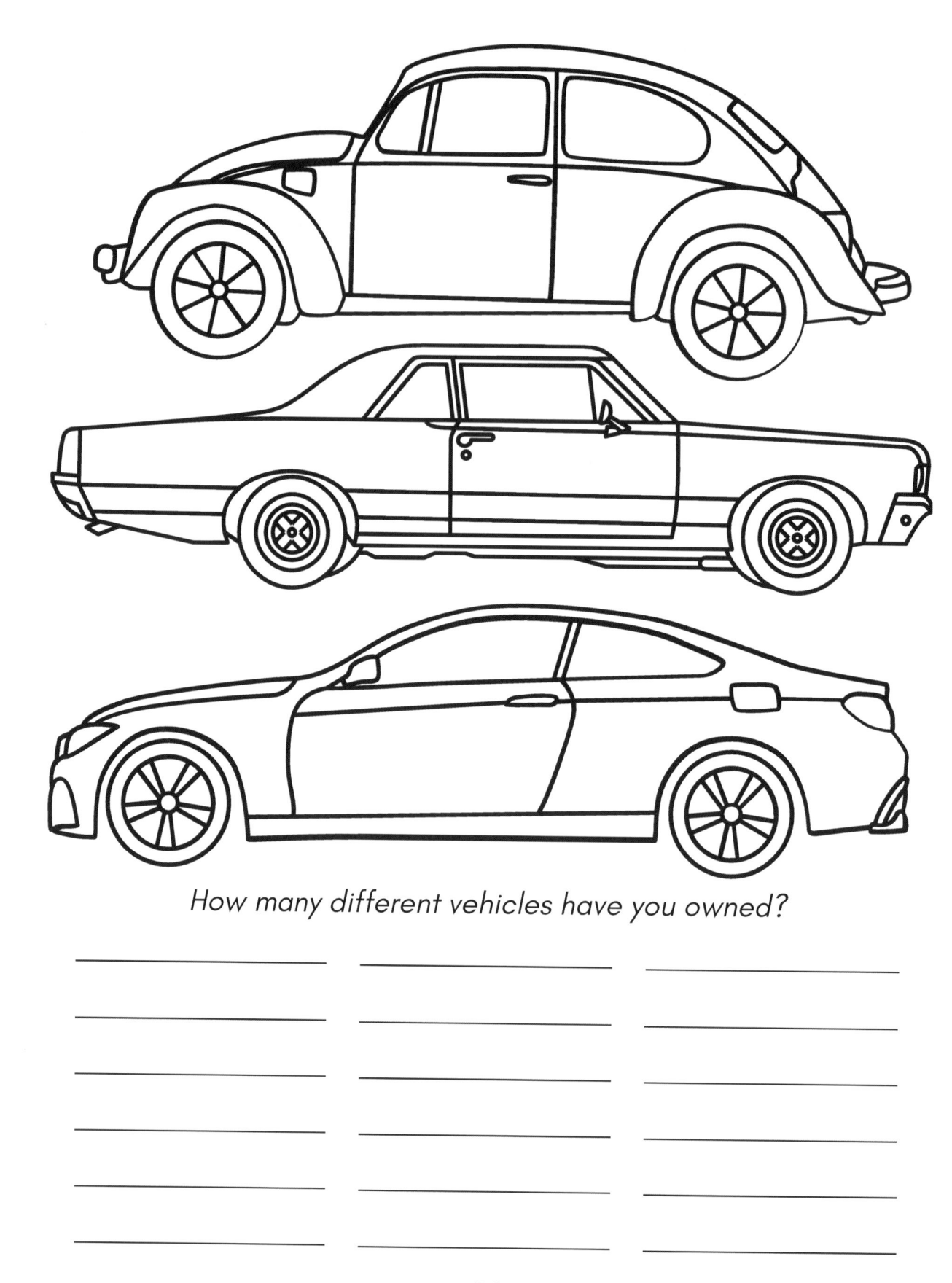

_____ _____ _____

_____ _____ _____

_____ _____ _____

_____ _____ _____

_____ _____ _____

_____ _____ _____

In 1872, Walter Scott pioneered the first diner concept by selling food from a horse-pulled wagon with walk-up service windows in Providence, Rhode Island.

Did you have a favorite diner? If so, where was it?

PRESIDENTS

Review the pictures of the presidents elected in your lifetime. Color in the ones you or your parents voted for.

Dwight D. Eisenhower
1953 – 1961

John F. Kennedy
1961 – 1963

Lyndon B. Johnson
1963 – 1969

Richard Nixon
1969 – 1974

Gerald Ford
1974 – 1977

Jimmy Carter
1977 – 1981

Ronald Reagan
1981 – 1989

George H.W. Bush
1989 – 1993

Bill Clinton
1993 – 2001

George W. Bush
2001 – 2009

Barack Obama
2009 – 2017

Donald Trump
2017 – 2021
2025 – 2029

Joe Biden
2021

-28-

NOSTALGIA NOTES

Fill in the blanks first, then go back and read your story aloud.

Way back in _____, I landed my first job as a
(favorite year)
_____. It was as exhilarating as my first roller coaster ride
(first job)
at _____. Every day, I'd hop into my trusty _____,
(first vacation spot)   (first car)
with _____ by my side, barking along to the tunes
(first pet's name)
of _____. Work was a far cry from _____,
(favorite song)   (favorite hobby)
but it paid for my _____ addiction and movie nights
(favorite dessert)
featuring _____.
(favorite actor/actress)
One evening, after a long shift, I mustered the courage to ask
_____ out on a date. We planned to meet at
(first date's name)
_____. I put on my _____, which I thought was
(favorite restaurant)   (item of clothing)
the epitome of cool. Unfortunately, the _____ was so tight;
(article of clothing)
it made sitting down a risky business! During dinner, I tried to
impress with stories about my _____, but
(a life accomplishment)
accidentally spat out a piece of _____ right onto the
(favorite food)
_____. Despite the mishap, we ended up having a blast,
(an object in a kitchen)
laughing like we were characters in _____.
(your favorite book)
It was a night to remember!

Remember When

Instead of focusing on the year you were born, let's focus on the years you remember! While the year you were born is important, it's the years after that defined who you are today. Let's take a trip along the journey and discover why you are who you are.

1967 - **You turned 12**
The Summer of Love was in full swing, with thousands of young people converging to promote peace, love, and music.

What do you remember feeling or thinking about this cultural revolution when you were a teenager?

....

....

....

1973 - **You turned 18**
The Paris Peace Accords were signed in January 1973, officially ending U.S. involvement in the Vietnam War.

How did you feel about the conclusion of the Vietnam war as you were entering adulthood?

....

....

....

....

REMEMBER WHEN

1976 - You turned 21
Jimmy Carter, a Democrat and former Governor of Georgia, defeated incumbent Republican President Gerald Ford in a close election.

What were your thoughts or feelings about this election as you celebrated turning 21?

1980 - You turned 25
The death of John Lennon: The former Beatles member was tragically murdered in New York City.

As you turned 25, how do you remember feeling when you learned of John Lennon's death?

1985 - You turned 30
The release of Microsoft Windows 1.0: This marked the beginning of the Windows operating system.

When did you first encounter a personal computer, and how did you imagine it would change the future?

Remember When

1995 - You turned 40
The O.J. Simpson Trial: The trial of O.J. Simpson for the murders of Nicole Brown Simpson and Ron Goldman captivated the nation.

Reflect on how you felt about the O.J. Simpson trial and its verdict.

....

....

....

....

2005 - You turned 50
YouTube was launched in February, revolutionizing how people consume and share video content online.

Can you recall your first experience with YouTube or what you thought about it when it first emerged?

....

....

....

....

2015 - You turned 60
The rise of streaming services: 2015 saw the continued growth of streaming services like Netflix and Spotify.

Reflect on how you used to watch movies and listen to music.

....

....

Remember When

2025 - You turn 70!

As you celebrate this milestone, what recent event has given you hope or excitement for the future?

_____

_____

_____

_____

More Milestone Memories

Make a note of any other major events or years that are seared in your memory as significant.

_____

_____

_____

_____

_____

_____

REFLECTIONS

Reflect on a moment of significant change in your life. If you could write to yourself just before this event, what insights or comfort would you offer?

Reflect on your career path or life's work. What would you say to your younger self about following their dreams and the realities of the working world?

Recall a time you took a significant risk. Encourage your younger self about the value of risk-taking and the growth that comes from stepping out of your comfort zones.

REFLECTIONS

Ponder on the love and relationships in your life. Offer your younger self wisdom about love, loss, and the enduring nature of true connections.

Think of a joyous milestone in your life. Tell your younger self about the happiness that lies ahead and the importance of savoring those moments.

Acknowledge the societal changes you've witnessed. Write about how these changes have shaped your perspective and the world you've navigated.

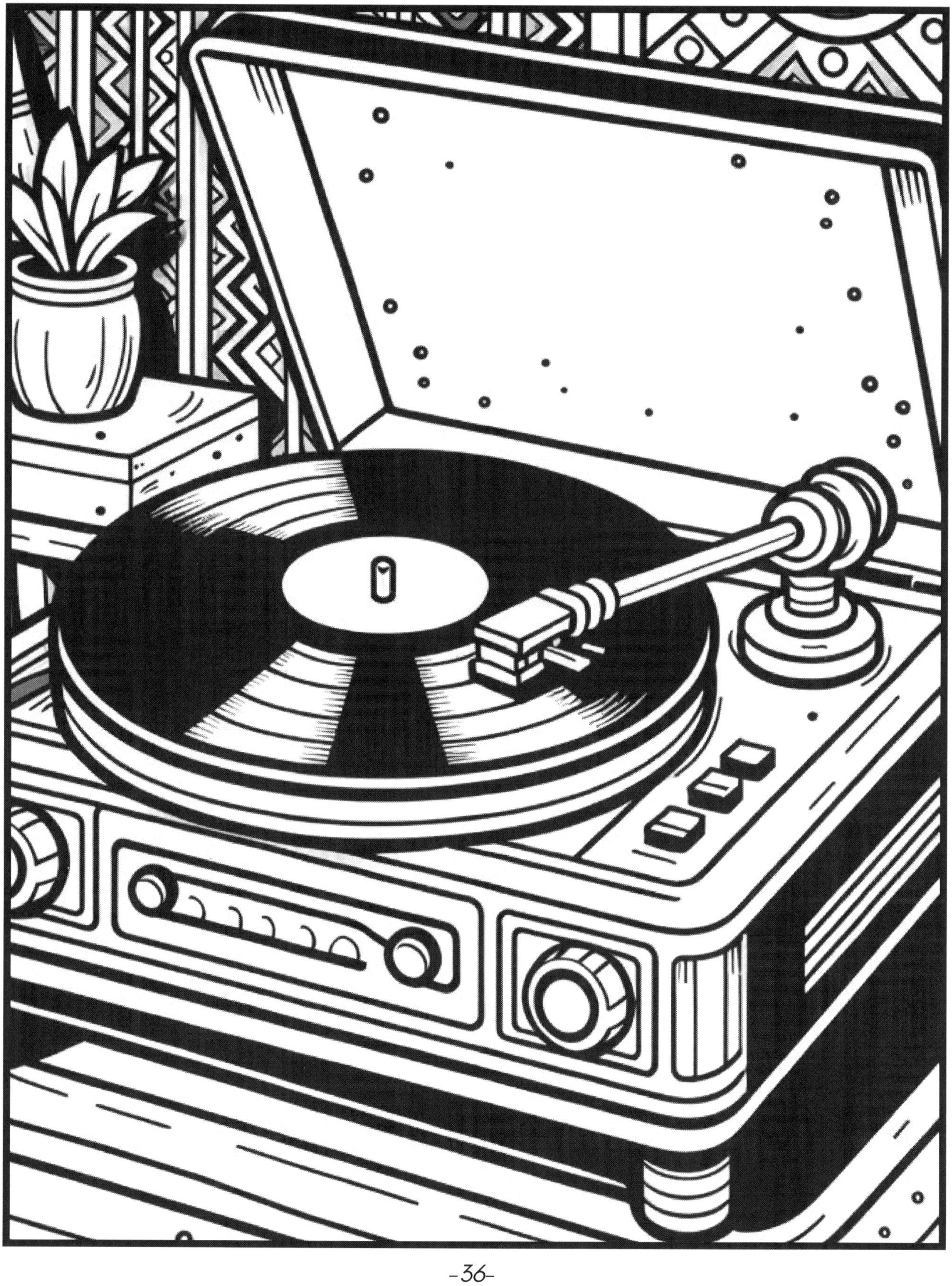

CHECK YOUR ANSWERS

The Price is Right

Check your answers.

Avg. Wage/Year
a) $4,137 ✓
b) $2,000
c) $8,500

New Home
a) $5,500
b) $15,300
c) $10,950 ✓

Loaf of Bread
a) $0.50
b) $1.00
c) $0.18 ✓

Gold/Ounce
a) $200
b) $35 ✓
c) $10

Gallon of Gas
a) $0.23 ✓
b) $0.55
c) $0.10

Harvard Tuition
a) $2,000
b) $400
c) $800 ✓

Dozen Eggs
a) $0.10
b) $0.27 ✓
c) $1.75

Postage Stamp
a) $0.05
b) $0.03 ✓
c) $0.10

A Movie Ticket
a) $1.25
b) $0.10
c) $0.75 ✓

*costs are average estimates

YOUNGER OR OLDER?

Check your answers.

		Younger	Older
1	Microwave oven	✓ 1945	○
2	Tupperware	✓ 1946	○
3	Rubiks Cube	○	✓ 1974
4	Mr. Potato Head	✓ 1949	○
5	Color TV	✓ 1953	○
6	Frisbee	○	✓ 1957
7	Helicopter	✓ 1939	○
8	Hula Hoop	○	✓ 1957
9	Laser	○	✓ 1960
10	Car Seat Belts	✓ 1855	○
11	Barbie Doll	○	✓ 1959
12	Credit Card	✓ 1950	○
13	Monopoly Board Game	✓ 1902	○
14	Electric Guitar	✓ 1932	○
15	Sliced Bread	✓ 1928	○

WORD SEARCH

N	S	Y	N	X	M	V	B	E	H
J	P	H	S	A	C	I	E	Y	U
U	U	T	P	E	T	C	A	N	L
K	T	R	E	L	C	W	T	A	A
E	N	A	L	Y	G	A	L	T	H
B	I	C	V	N	B	H	E	O	O
O	K	C	I	I	U	E	S	P	O
X	J	M	S	V	E	C	A	E	P
T	E	L	E	V	I	S	I	O	N
H	K	C	O	T	S	D	O	O	W

ELVIS   **NATO**   **PEACE**
MCCARTHY   **WOODSTOCK**   **HULA HOOP**
TELEVISION   **BEATLES**   **VINYL**
HEMINGWAY   **JUKEBOX**   **SPUTNIK**

GUESS THE MOVIE

Check your answers.

"You see, in this world, there's two kinds of people, my friend: Those with loaded guns, and those who dig. You dig." — The Good, the Bad and the Ugly, 1966

"I coulda been a contender." — On the Waterfront, 1954

"Hasta la vista, baby." — Terminator 2: Judgment Day, 1991

"Life moves pretty fast. If you don't stop and look around once in a while, you could miss it." — Ferris Bueller's Day Off, 1986

"You talkin' to me?" — Taxi Driver, 1976

"If you build it, they will come." — Field of Dreams, 1988

"Here's to you, Mrs. Robinson." — The Graduate, 1967

"What we've got here is failure to communicate." — Cool Hand Luke, 1967

"Gentlemen, you can't fight in here! This is the War Room!" — Dr. Strangelove, 1964

Born in 1955

Check your answers.

		True	False
1	**Bruce Willis**	✓	○
2	**Kevin Costner**	✓	○
3	**Bill Murray**	○	✓
4	**Bill Nye**	✓	○
5	**Stevie Wonder**	○	✓
6	**Whoopi Goldberg**	✓	○
7	**Sharon Stone**	○	✓
8	**Steve Jobs**	✓	○
9	**Liam Neeson**	○	✓
10	**Whoopie Goldberg**	✓	○
11	**Reba McEntire**	✓	○
12	**Eddie Van Halen**	✓	○
13	**Hillary Clinton**	○	✓
14	**Dolly Parton**	○	✓
15	**John Grisham**	✓	○

1950s SLANG

Check your answers.

1. **Fat city** — A state of great success
2. **Burn rubber** — To drive away quickly
3. **Knuckle sandwich** — A playful threat of a punch
4. **Made in the shade** — Suggesting someone has it easy
5. **Pad** — A house or home
6. **Blast** — Having a great time
7. **Shoot the breeze** — To chat casually without purpose
8. **Out to lunch** — Someone who's clueless
9. **Peepers** — Glasses or spectacles
10. **Real gone** — Very much in love
11. **Jet** — To leave quickly
12. **Square** — Describing someone as unhip
13. **Drag** — Something that's boring
14. **Razz my berries** — To excite or impress someone
15. **Flip your wig** — To become very excited or go crazy

-43-

Finish the Sentence

Check your answers.

"You ain't nothin' but a hound dog, **cryin' all the time.**"
- Elvis Presley (1956)

"Imagine there's no heaven, **it's easy if you try.**"
- John Lennon, "Imagine" (1971)

"All you need is love, **love is all you need.**" - The Beatles (1967)

"Hey Jude, don't **make it bad.** Take a sad song and make it better."
- The Beatles (1968)

"You're so vain, you probably **think this song is about you.**"
- Carly Simon (1972)

"We will, we will **rock you.**" - Queen, "We Will Rock You" (1977)

"Don't stop believing, **hold on to that feeling**." - Journey (1981)

"Every breath you take, **every move you make**, I'll be watching you."
- The Police, "Every Breath You Take" (1983)

"Wake me up **before you go-go**, don't leave me hanging on like a yo-yo."
- Wham! (1984)

"I want to dance with somebody, **I want to feel the heat** with somebody."
- Whitney Houston (1987)

TIMELINE

Pause to thoughtfully record a few of the significant milestones and events that have shaped your journey.

Date: Event/Memory:

Date: Event/Memory:

Date: Event/Memory:

Date: Event/Memory:

Date: Event/Memory:

TIMELINE

Date: Event/Memory:

Date: Event/Memory:

Date: Event/Memory:

Date: Event/Memory:

Date: Event/Memory:

TIMELINE

Date:　　　　　　　Event/Memory:

Date:　　　　　　　Event/Memory:

Date:　　　　　　　Event/Memory:

Date:　　　　　　　Event/Memory:

Date:　　　　　　　Event/Memory:

TIMELINE

Date: Event/Memory:

Date: Event/Memory:

Date: Event/Memory:

Date: Event/Memory:

Date: Event/Memory:

TIMELINE

Date: Event/Memory:

Date: Event/Memory:

Date: Event/Memory:

Date: Event/Memory:

Date: Event/Memory:

GRATITUDE

With 70 years worth of blessings, take a moment now to fill in your year of birth with the first things that spring to mind for which you are deeply grateful.

19

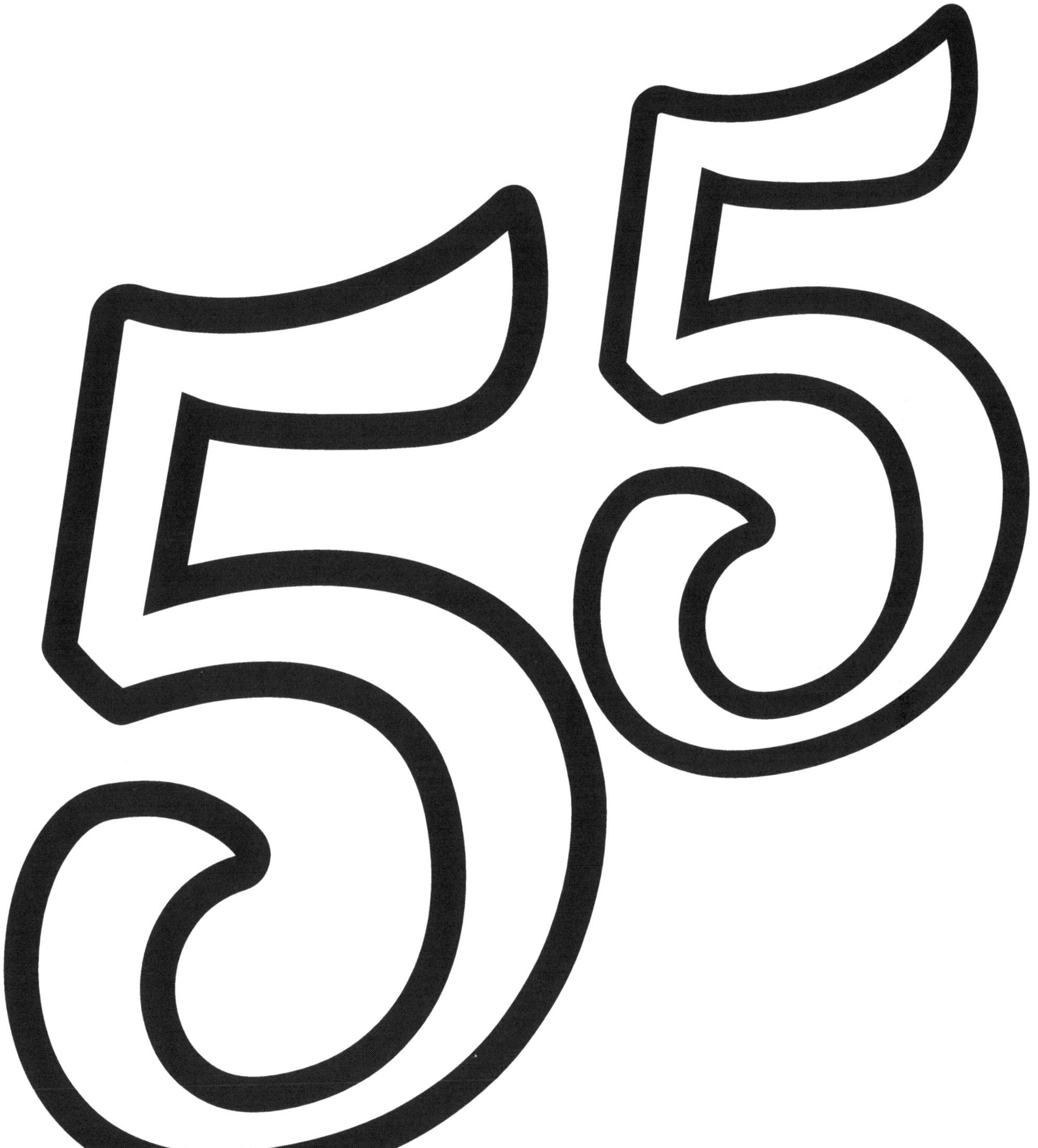

The Future

Anticipating the future, fill in the year 2025 with any goals and dreams that still remain on your bucket list.

20

25

Notes

Notes

Made in the USA
Columbia, SC
28 April 2025